Introduction

Greetings,

I'm Brian Driggs, and I'm thrilled to welcome you to "The 7 Pillars of SEO." As the owner of Social Funnel Marketing, I've spent years immersed in the dynamic world of digital marketing, and I'm excited to share with you the insights and strategies that have propelled businesses to new heights.

In this book, we embark on a journey that demystifies the art of Search Engine Optimization (SEO). Together, we'll explore the seven fundamental pillars that underpin online success. Whether you're a business owner aiming to enhance your digital presence or someone eager to dive into the world of SEO, this guide is your trusted companion.

I've seen firsthand the transformative power of SEO, and I'm passionate about helping you unlock its potential. These seven pillars aren't just concepts; they are the building blocks of a robust online strategy that can elevate your website's visibility, attract organic traffic, and drive conversions.

Throughout this book, I'll share practical advice, real-world examples, and actionable steps that you can implement immediately. SEO doesn't have to be a mysterious and daunting realm; it can be your greatest ally in the digital landscape.

So, whether you're new to SEO or looking to refine your existing strategy, join me on this journey as we uncover the secrets of "The 7 Pillars of SEO." Together, we'll empower your online presence and redefine your digital success.

Let's dive in and unlock the incredible potential of SEO.

Sincerely,
Brian Driggs

BRIAN DRIGGS

Owner, Social Funnel Marketing

PILLAR 1: THE POWER OF QUALITY CONTENT IN SEO

In the vast digital landscape, the adage "Content is King" has never rung truer. Quality content is the bedrock upon which successful SEO strategies are built. In this chapter, we will explore the profound impact that quality content has on your website's search engine rankings and how you, as a small business owner or SEO enthusiast, can harness this power to your advantage.

The Significance of Quality Content

Imagine your website as a digital storefront. Your content is the signage, the showcase, and the sales pitch all rolled into one. It's not just about attracting visitors; it's about captivating them, providing value, and leaving a lasting impression. Here's why quality content is paramount:

1. **User Satisfaction**: When users visit your website, they're seeking information, solutions, or entertainment. Quality content delivers on these expectations, leaving users satisfied with their visit.

2. **Engagement and Retention**: Well-crafted content keeps visitors engaged, encourages them to explore your site further, and increases the time they spend on your pages. This not only reduces bounce rates but also signals to search engines that your content is valuable.

3. **Establishing Authority**: Authoritative content positions you as an expert in your field. When users trust your content, they're more likely to trust your products or services.

4. **Backlinks and Sharing**: Other websites are more likely to link to and share content that is informative, well-researched, or

entertaining. This helps build a strong backlink profile, a vital component of SEO.

Understanding User Intent

Before diving into content creation, it's essential to grasp user intent. User intent is the reason behind a user's online search. It can generally be categorized into three types:

1. **Informational Intent**: Users seek information or answers to questions. Content catering to this intent includes how-to guides, tutorials, and informative articles.

2. **Navigational Intent**: Users want to find a specific website or page. They often use branded keywords or phrases. Ensuring your site is easily navigable and ranks well for your brand-related terms is key.

3. **Transactional Intent**: Users are ready to make a purchase or take a specific action. Product descriptions, reviews, and checkout pages cater to this intent.

Aligning your content with user intent is pivotal. Google's algorithms analyze user behavior to determine the relevance of your content. If users frequently click on your page but quickly return to the search results (a high bounce rate), it signals to Google that your content may not align with their intent.

The Role of Keywords in Quality Content

Keywords are the bridges between your content and user intent. They are the terms and phrases users type into search engines to find what they're looking for. Here's how keywords fit into the equation:

1. **Keyword Research**: It all begins with keyword research. Start by brainstorming relevant keywords related to your business or niche. Consider what your target audience might search for. Use tools like Google Keyword Planner, SEMrush, or Ahrefs to expand your keyword list.

2. **Long-Tail Keywords**: While broad keywords have high search volumes, they also come with fierce competition. Long-tail keywords, which are more specific phrases, often have less competition and can attract highly targeted traffic.

3. **Assessing Keyword Competition**: Not all keywords are equal. Some are easier to rank for than others due to lower competition. Assess keyword competition to determine which ones are realistic targets for your website.

4. **Keyword Optimization**: Once you've selected your target keywords, it's time to strategically integrate them into your content. Ensure they appear in the title, headings, and body of your content. However, be mindful of keyword stuffing, which can harm your rankings.

Crafting Exceptional Content

Now that you understand user intent and have a list of targeted keywords, it's time to create content that stands out. Exceptional content sets you apart and keeps visitors coming back. Here's how to craft it:

1. **In-Depth Information**: Comprehensive, well-researched content tends to perform better in search results. Dive deep into your topics and provide information that isn't readily available elsewhere. Be the go-to source for your niche.

2. **Engaging Writing**: Quality content is more than facts and figures; it's about engaging your audience. Use storytelling, anecdotes, and a conversational tone when appropriate. Make your content enjoyable to read.

3. **Visual Elements**: Text alone isn't always enough. Incorporate visuals such as images, infographics, and videos to enhance your content's appeal and clarify complex concepts.

4. **Clear Structure**: Organize your content logically with headings and subheadings. This not only makes it more reader-

friendly but also helps search engines understand your content's structure.

5. **Originality**: Plagiarism is a strict no-no. Ensure your content is original and offers a unique perspective on the topic. Duplicate content can harm your SEO efforts.

Content Optimization Beyond Text

While written content is central, SEO encompasses more than just words. To offer a holistic user experience, consider these elements:

1. **Image Optimization**: Images are an integral part of web content. Optimize them for web use by compressing without sacrificing quality. Include descriptive alt text to enhance accessibility and SEO.

2. **Video Content**: Video has become increasingly popular. Create engaging video content and optimize it with relevant keywords and descriptions. YouTube, owned by Google, is the second-largest search engine, emphasizing the importance of video SEO.

3. **Interactive Content**: Experiment with interactive elements such as quizzes, surveys, calculators, and interactive infographics. These can engage users and keep them on your site longer.

4. **Content Updates**: Don't let your content stagnate. Regularly revisit and update your existing content. This shows search engines that your site is fresh and up-to-date, enhancing your rankings.

Analytics and User Feedback

Creating quality content is an ongoing process that requires constant refinement. To improve your content and better cater to your audience, you need to gather data and feedback:

1. **Analytics**: Monitor user behavior on your site through

tools like Google Analytics. Pay attention to metrics like bounce rate, time on page, and conversion rates. These metrics provide valuable insights into how users interact with your content.

2. **User Surveys**: Conduct surveys to collect direct feedback from your audience. What do they like, dislike, or wish to see improved? User input can guide your content strategy.

3. **Comments and Social Engagement**: Engage with users through comments on your site and on social media platforms. Address their questions and concerns promptly. Interacting with your audience not only enhances user experience but also builds a community around your brand.

In the ever-evolving realm of SEO, quality content remains the unshakable foundation upon which successful rankings are built. Small business owners and aspiring SEO enthusiasts can harness the power of quality content to not only attract visitors but also engage, educate, and convert them into loyal customers. Remember, SEO is not a one-time effort; it's an ongoing journey of learning, adapting, and refining your content strategy to meet the ever-changing demands of users and search engines alike.

PILLAR 2: MASTERING KEYWORD RESEARCH AND USAGE IN SEO

In the ever-competitive digital landscape, keyword research and strategic usage are your compass to navigate the vast sea of online content. This chapter is dedicated to unraveling the art and science of keyword research and how effectively incorporating keywords into your content can significantly impact your website's search engine rankings.

The Essence of Keywords in SEO

Keywords are the language of search engines. They are the phrases and terms that users type into search bars when seeking answers, products, or services. Understanding keywords and harnessing their potential can be a game-changer in your SEO strategy. Here's why they matter:

1. **User Connection**: Keywords are your direct link to user intent. When you align your content with relevant keywords, you're more likely to attract users actively seeking what you offer.

2. **Visibility**: By optimizing for specific keywords, you increase the likelihood of your content appearing in search engine results pages (SERPs). This increased visibility can lead to more organic traffic.

3. **Competition Analysis**: Keywords can offer insights into your competition. By analyzing which keywords your competitors target, you can identify opportunities and gaps in your own SEO strategy.

Unveiling the Keyword Research Process

Effective keyword research is both art and science. It requires a systematic approach to uncover the keywords that resonate with your target audience. Let's explore this process step by step:

1. **Brainstorm Relevant Keywords**: Begin by brainstorming keywords related to your business, products, or niche. Think about what your potential customers might search for. This initial list will serve as a foundation.

2. **Use Keyword Research Tools**: Leverage keyword research tools like Google Keyword Planner, SEMrush, Ahrefs, or Moz. These tools provide valuable insights into keyword search volumes, competition levels, and related keyword suggestions.

3. **Long-Tail Keywords**: Don't solely focus on high-volume, broad keywords. Long-tail keywords, which are more specific and often less competitive, can be goldmines of targeted traffic. They cater to users with very specific queries.

4. **Assess Keyword Competition**: Gauge the competition for your chosen keywords. Highly competitive keywords may require more time and effort to rank for. Balancing high and low competition keywords in your strategy can be effective.

Strategically Integrating Keywords

Once you've curated your list of keywords, it's time to seamlessly weave them into your content. Keyword integration should feel natural and not disrupt the flow of your writing. Here's how to achieve that:

1. **Title Optimization**: Place your chosen keyword in the title of your content whenever possible. The title is the first thing both users and search engines see.

2. **Heading Tags**: Use headings (H1, H2, H3, etc.) to structure your content. Include keywords in headings to signal the importance of certain topics to search engines and improve readability for users.

3. **In-Content Usage**: Sprinkle your keywords naturally

throughout your content, including in the body text, but avoid overstuffing. The goal is to provide valuable information to readers, not simply to rank for keywords.

4. **Image Alt Text**: Don't forget about images. Include descriptive alt text for images, incorporating relevant keywords where appropriate. This practice enhances both accessibility and SEO.

5. **Meta Tags**: Optimize meta tags, including the meta title and meta description, to include keywords. These elements are displayed in search results and can influence click-through rates.

Keyword Research and User Intent

While keyword research is crucial, it should always be aligned with user intent. Remember that the ultimate goal is to provide value to users. Here's how keyword research and user intent intersect:

1. **Understanding User Needs**: Use keyword research to understand what your audience is searching for. What questions are they asking? What problems are they trying to solve? Cater your content to address these needs.

2. **Answering User Queries**: When crafting content, think about how you can answer user queries comprehensively. Don't just target keywords; aim to provide valuable information that satisfies user intent.

3. **Long-Tail Keywords**: Long-tail keywords often indicate specific user intent. For example, someone searching for "best running shoes for marathons" has a clear intent. Tailor your content to cater to these specific queries.

Tracking and Adapting Your Keyword Strategy

Keyword research isn't a one-and-done task. It's an ongoing process that requires monitoring and adaptation. Here's how to ensure your keyword strategy remains effective:

1. **Regular Auditing**: Periodically audit your existing content to ensure that keywords are still relevant and aligned with user intent. Update content as needed to reflect current trends and user queries.

2. **Monitor Rankings**: Keep track of how your content ranks for target keywords. Tools like SEMrush or Ahrefs can help you monitor your ranking positions and identify opportunities for improvement.

3. **Competitor Analysis**: Continue to analyze your competitors' keyword strategies. Are there new keywords they are targeting? Can you identify gaps in your own strategy based on their successes or shortcomings?

Keywords are the foundation of your SEO strategy. By understanding user intent, conducting thorough keyword research, and skillfully integrating keywords into your content, you empower your website to attract organic traffic and rank higher in search engine results. Remember that SEO is a dynamic field, and staying up-to-date with the latest keyword trends and user preferences is key to maintaining your competitive edge.

PILLAR 3: ON-PAGE OPTIMIZATION: YOUR KEY TO SEO SUCCESS**

On-Page Optimization is the fine-tuning of individual web pages to maximize their visibility and relevance to search engines. In this chapter, we'll explore the intricacies of on-page optimization, providing you with the knowledge and techniques needed to ensure that your web pages are primed for SEO success.

The Crucial Role of On-Page Optimization

Imagine your website as a library, and each web page as a book. On-Page Optimization is like crafting the perfect cover, title, and index for each book, making them not only appealing but also easy for readers (search engines) to understand. Here's why it's crucial:

1. **Improved Visibility**: On-Page Optimization enhances your web pages' visibility in search engine results pages (SERPs), increasing the chances of attracting organic traffic.

2. **Relevance to Search Queries**: By optimizing your pages for specific keywords and user intent, you ensure that your content aligns with what users are searching for.

3. **Better User Experience**: On-Page Optimization often leads to improved user experience, as well-structured and organized content is more accessible and user-friendly.

The Core Elements of On-Page Optimization

On-Page Optimization encompasses several core elements that should be addressed for each web page. Let's break them down:

1. **Title Tags**: The title tag is arguably the most critical on-page element. It appears as the clickable headline in search results and

sets the stage for what the page is about. Optimize it by including your target keyword and creating a compelling, informative title.

2. **Meta Descriptions**: Meta descriptions provide a brief summary of what a page is about. While they don't directly impact rankings, they influence click-through rates. Craft engaging meta descriptions that entice users to click on your page.

3. **URL Structure**: Create clean, descriptive URLs that include keywords when relevant. A well-structured URL can convey the topic of your page to both users and search engines.

4. **Headings (H1, H2, H3, etc.)**: Use heading tags to structure your content logically. The H1 tag should include the main topic or keyword, while subheadings (H2, H3, etc.) organize content into sections.

5. **Keyword Optimization**: Strategically include your target keyword(s) in the page's content. Ensure natural usage that enhances the user experience rather than disrupts it.

6. **Content Quality and Length**: High-quality, informative content tends to perform better. Aim for in-depth, comprehensive content that thoroughly covers the topic. Longer content often outranks shorter pieces, but the focus should always be on quality.

7. **Internal Linking**: Include relevant internal links within your content. Internal links help users navigate your site and distribute link equity across your pages.

8. **External Links**: If relevant, include authoritative external links in your content. Outbound links to trusted sources can enhance your page's credibility.

9. **Image Optimization**: Optimize images by compressing them without sacrificing quality. Use descriptive alt text that includes keywords to improve accessibility and SEO.

10. **Mobile-Friendliness**: Ensure that your web page is responsive and displays correctly on mobile devices. Google

considers mobile-friendliness a ranking factor.

11. **Page Speed**: Faster-loading pages are preferred by both users and search engines. Optimize your page speed by reducing unnecessary code, compressing images, and using browser caching.

On-Page SEO Best Practices

To excel in on-page optimization, consider these best practices:

1. **Unique and Valuable Content**: Create content that stands out from the competition. Offer unique insights, solutions, or perspectives that benefit your audience.

2. **Keyword Variations**: Don't rely solely on one keyword. Use variations and synonyms naturally to capture a broader range of search queries.

3. **Avoid Keyword Stuffing**: While it's essential to include keywords, avoid overloading your content with them. Maintain a natural and reader-friendly flow.

4. **Regular Updates**: Periodically revisit and update your content to keep it fresh and accurate. This signals to search engines that your content is up-to-date.

5. **User Experience**: Prioritize user experience. Ensure that your content is easy to read and navigate, with a clear hierarchy of information.

6. **Schema Markup**: Implement schema markup to provide search engines with additional context about your content. This can result in rich snippets in search results.

On-Page Optimization is the art of fine-tuning your individual web pages for maximum SEO impact. By optimizing title tags, meta descriptions, content, and other on-page elements, you pave the way for improved search engine rankings and user experience. Remember that SEO is an ongoing journey, and regularly auditing and optimizing your pages is key to maintaining and enhancing your online presence.

PILLAR 4: BUILDING BACKLINKS AND AUTHORITY IN SEO

Backlinks, also known as inbound links, and authority are essential components of SEO success. In this chapter, we'll uncover the significance of backlinks, how they contribute to your website's authority, and strategies for building a strong backlink profile.

Understanding the Power of Backlinks

Imagine backlinks as endorsements from other websites. Each link to your site is like a vote of confidence, indicating to search engines that your content is valuable and trustworthy. Here's why backlinks are crucial:

1. **Improved Search Rankings**: Websites with a robust backlink profile tend to rank higher in search engine results. Backlinks signal to search engines that your content is authoritative and relevant.

2. **Enhanced Credibility**: Backlinks from reputable websites boost your site's credibility and authority in your niche or industry.

3. **Increased Traffic**: Quality backlinks can drive referral traffic from other websites to yours, expanding your audience.

Quality vs. Quantity: The Backlink Dilemma

Not all backlinks are created equal. Quality far outweighs quantity when it comes to backlinks. A single high-quality backlink from a reputable site can have a more significant impact than numerous low-quality links. Here's what distinguishes a quality backlink:

1. **Relevance**: A quality backlink comes from a website or page

that is relevant to your content. For example, if you run a fitness blog, a backlink from a reputable fitness equipment manufacturer is highly relevant.

2. **Authority**: Websites with high domain authority, often measured on a scale of 1-100, pass more authority to your site through backlinks. Getting links from authoritative sites is valuable.

3. **Editorial Context**: A backlink within the context of an article or content piece is more valuable than a link in a sidebar or footer.

4. **Natural Link Building**: Backlinks that are earned naturally due to the quality and relevance of your content are more valuable than paid or spammy links.

Effective Backlink Building Strategies

Building a strong backlink profile requires a well-thought-out strategy. Here are some effective strategies to acquire quality backlinks:

1. **Create Exceptional Content**: Content that stands out naturally attracts backlinks. Craft high-quality, informative, and engaging content that others want to reference and share.

2. **Guest Blogging**: Contribute guest posts to authoritative websites in your niche. Include relevant backlinks to your own content within the guest post.

3. **Broken Link Building**: Identify broken links on authoritative websites in your niche. Reach out to the site owner, inform them of the broken link, and suggest replacing it with a link to your relevant content.

4. **Outreach and Networking**: Build relationships with influencers, bloggers, and industry leaders. Outreach to them and suggest collaborations, interviews, or content sharing opportunities that can lead to backlinks.

5. **Social Media Promotion**: Share your content on social media platforms to increase its visibility. While social shares themselves aren't direct backlinks, they can lead to others discovering and linking to your content.

6. **Resource Page Linking**: Find resource pages or lists within your niche that curate helpful content. Reach out to the page owner and suggest your content for inclusion.

7. **Ego Baiting**: Create content that features or mentions influencers, businesses, or products in your industry. Inform those mentioned, and they may link to your content.

8. **HARO (Help a Reporter Out)**: Sign up for HARO to respond to journalist queries within your expertise. If your response gets featured in an article, it often includes a backlink to your website.

Measuring Backlink Success

Tracking the success of your backlink-building efforts is essential. Use tools like Ahrefs, SEMrush, or Moz to monitor your backlinks, their quality, and their impact on your rankings. Pay attention to metrics like Domain Authority, referring domains, and anchor text diversity.

Avoid Common Backlink Pitfalls

While building backlinks, be cautious of the following pitfalls:

1. **Buying Links**: Purchasing backlinks is against Google's guidelines and can lead to penalties.

2. **Low-Quality Directories**: Submitting your site to low-quality or spammy directories can harm your SEO. Focus on reputable directories if you choose to use them.

3. **Irrelevant Links**: Avoid acquiring links from irrelevant websites or those with low authority. These can have a negative impact on your backlink profile.

Backlinks are the building blocks of authority in the world of SEO. By focusing on acquiring quality backlinks from relevant and authoritative sources, you enhance your website's credibility and improve its search engine rankings. Remember that backlink building is an ongoing process, and continually seeking opportunities to earn valuable links will solidify your website's authority in your niche or industry.

PILLAR 5: MASTERING TECHNICAL SEO FOR WEBSITE SUCCESS

Technical SEO focuses on the behind-the-scenes aspects of your website that impact its visibility and performance in search engine results. In this chapter, we'll uncover the critical components of technical SEO and how optimizing them can boost your website's rankings.

The Significance of Technical SEO

Imagine technical SEO as the infrastructure of your website—the unseen framework that ensures everything runs smoothly. It's vital for the following reasons:

1. **Indexability**: Technical SEO ensures that search engines can easily crawl and index your website's pages, making your content accessible to users.

2. **Site Speed**: Fast-loading pages not only provide a better user experience but also influence search rankings. Technical optimizations can improve your site's speed.

3. **Mobile Friendliness**: As mobile devices become the primary means of internet access, mobile-friendliness is crucial for SEO. Technical SEO includes making your site responsive and mobile-friendly.

Key Components of Technical SEO

To excel in technical SEO, you need to address several critical components:

1. **Website Architecture**: A well-structured website with clear navigation helps search engines understand your content's hierarchy. Use logical categories, menus, and internal linking.

2. **XML Sitemaps**: Create and submit XML sitemaps to search engines. Sitemaps provide a roadmap of your website's pages, ensuring they get indexed.

3. **Robots.txt**: Use a robots.txt file to instruct search engine bots on which pages to crawl and which to exclude. This file helps control indexing.

4. **Website Speed**: Optimize your website for speed by compressing images, minifying code, using browser caching, and choosing reliable hosting.

5. **Mobile Optimization**: Ensure your website is mobile-friendly and responsive. Google uses mobile-first indexing, making mobile optimization crucial.

6. **SSL Certificate**: Secure your website with an SSL certificate. Google gives preference to secure sites, and it's essential for user trust.

7. **Structured Data Markup**: Implement structured data (schema markup) to provide search engines with additional context about your content. This can result in rich snippets in search results.

8. **Canonical Tags**: Use canonical tags to indicate the preferred version of duplicate content. This helps prevent issues with duplicate content penalties.

9. **404 Errors and Redirects**: Monitor and fix 404 errors (broken links). Implement proper redirects (301 redirects) for pages that have moved or changed URLs.

10. **Site Search Functionality**: If your site has a search feature, ensure it functions correctly and returns relevant results.

Auditing and Optimizing Technical SEO

Auditing your website's technical SEO is essential to identify and address issues. Here's how to go about it:

1. **Use SEO Tools**: Tools like Google Search Console, SEMrush, Ahrefs, and Screaming Frog can help you identify technical issues and monitor your site's performance.

2. **Check for Crawling and Indexing Issues**: Ensure search engines can crawl and index your site. Check for crawl errors and blocked resources.

3. **Analyze Site Speed**: Use tools like Google PageSpeed Insights or GTmetrix to assess your site's speed. Address issues that slow down your site.

4. **Mobile-Friendly Testing**: Test your site's mobile-friendliness using Google's Mobile-Friendly Test tool. Make necessary adjustments if it's not mobile-friendly.

5. **Review SSL and Security**: Ensure your SSL certificate is active and correctly configured. Monitor your site for security vulnerabilities.

6. **Regular Audits**: Perform regular technical SEO audits to catch and fix issues promptly.

Common Technical SEO Pitfalls

While optimizing technical SEO, be aware of common pitfalls:

1. **Ignoring Mobile Optimization**: Neglecting mobile optimization can lead to lower rankings and a poor user experience.

2. **Overlooking Site Speed**: Slow-loading pages can frustrate users and harm rankings. Don't underestimate the importance of speed optimization.

3. **Not Implementing Structured Data**: Structured data markup can enhance your search results' appearance and click-through rates.

Technical SEO forms the foundation of your website's search

engine visibility. By addressing the technical aspects of your site, ensuring it's user-friendly, mobile-optimized, and error-free, you create a solid base for your content to shine. Regularly audit and maintain your technical SEO to stay competitive in the ever-evolving digital landscape.

PILLAR 6: DOMINATING LOCAL SEO FOR BUSINESS GROWTH

Local SEO focuses on optimizing your online presence to attract local customers. In this chapter, we'll delve into the importance of local SEO, the key components, and strategies to boost your business's visibility in local search results.

The Significance of Local SEO

Local SEO bridges the gap between online searchers and local businesses. Whether you run a brick-and-mortar store or offer local services, here's why local SEO matters:

1. **Increased Visibility**: Local SEO helps your business appear prominently in local search results, putting you in front of potential customers actively seeking nearby products or services.

2. **Improved Credibility**: A well-optimized Google My Business (GMB) profile and positive reviews can build trust and credibility in your local community.

3. **Foot Traffic**: For physical stores, local SEO can drive foot traffic, helping you attract customers who visit your location.

Key Components of Local SEO

To excel in local SEO, you need to address several critical components:

1. **Google My Business (GMB) Optimization**: Claim and optimize your GMB listing with accurate business information, including your name, address, phone number, and business hours. Add high-quality images and encourage customer reviews.

2. **Local Citations**: Ensure consistent business information

(NAP - Name, Address, Phone) across online directories, websites, and social platforms. Inaccurate citations can harm your local rankings.

3. **Online Reviews**: Encourage customers to leave reviews on your GMB profile and other review platforms like Yelp. Positive reviews boost your reputation and rankings.

4. **Local Content**: Create content tailored to local interests and events. Blog posts, articles, and landing pages with local keywords can attract local audiences.

5. **On-Page SEO**: Optimize your website's on-page elements with local keywords, including title tags, meta descriptions, and headings. Mention your location where relevant.

6. **Mobile Optimization**: Ensure your website is mobile-friendly, as many local searches occur on mobile devices.

7. **Local Link Building**: Build local backlinks from authoritative local websites, such as local news outlets, community organizations, and local blogs.

Strategies for Local SEO Success

Here are effective strategies to dominate local SEO:

1. **Keyword Research**: Research local keywords relevant to your business and incorporate them into your content and GMB profile.

2. **Localized Content**: Create content that speaks to local interests, events, and news. Highlight your involvement in the local community.

3. **Google My Business Posts**: Regularly post updates, promotions, and events on your GMB profile to keep it active and engaging.

4. **Local Schema Markup**: Implement schema markup with local business information to provide search engines with structured data about your business.

5. **Online Directories**: Ensure your business is listed accurately on major online directories, like Yelp, YellowPages, and TripAdvisor.

6. **Social Media Engagement**: Actively engage with your local audience on social media platforms. Respond to comments and messages promptly.

7. **Local Ads**: Consider running local ads on platforms like Google Ads and Facebook to target local audiences effectively.

Monitoring and Measuring Local SEO Success

Track the success of your local SEO efforts with the following metrics:

1. **Google My Business Insights**: Monitor GMB insights to track views, clicks, and customer actions on your profile.

2. **Local Rankings**: Use tools like Moz or SEMrush to track your local search rankings for relevant keywords.

3. **Review Monitoring**: Keep an eye on customer reviews and respond to them promptly, whether they are positive or negative.

Common Local SEO Pitfalls

Avoid these common pitfalls in local SEO:

1. **Inaccurate NAP Information**: Inconsistent or inaccurate business information can confuse both users and search engines.

2. **Ignoring Reviews**: Neglecting customer reviews, especially negative ones, can harm your reputation. Always respond professionally.

3. **Overlooking Mobile Optimization**: Many local searches occur on mobile devices, so mobile optimization is crucial.

Local SEO is the key to connecting with local customers and

growing your business. By optimizing your online presence with GMB, local citations, and localized content, you can enhance your visibility in local search results and build a loyal local customer base. Remember that local SEO requires ongoing maintenance and engagement with your community to maintain and improve your rankings.

PILLAR 7: ELEVATING USER EXPERIENCE AND CORE WEB VITALS FOR SEO

User Experience (UX) and Core Web Vitals play a crucial role in SEO success. In this chapter, we'll dive into the significance of a great user experience, how it impacts SEO, and how to optimize your website for Core Web Vitals.

The Vital Role of User Experience in SEO

Imagine UX as the journey your website visitors take. A positive experience can lead to higher rankings and more engaged users. Here's why UX matters:

1. **Reduced Bounce Rate**: A user-friendly website with fast-loading pages and easy navigation keeps visitors on your site longer, reducing bounce rates.

2. **Higher Engagement**: Engaged users are more likely to explore your content, leading to more page views and increased time on site.

3. **Improved Conversion Rates**: A seamless user experience can boost conversion rates, whether you aim to collect leads, make sales, or encourage other desired actions.

Understanding Core Web Vitals

Core Web Vitals are a set of user-focused metrics that measure the loading performance, interactivity, and visual stability of web pages. Google considers these metrics when ranking websites. The Core Web Vitals include:

1. **Largest Contentful Paint (LCP)**: Measures loading

performance by evaluating how long it takes for the largest element (e.g., an image or text block) to become visible.

2. **First Input Delay (FID)**: Measures interactivity by assessing how quickly a page responds to a user's first interaction, such as clicking a button.

3. **Cumulative Layout Shift (CLS)**: Measures visual stability by quantifying unexpected layout shifts during page loading.

Optimizing Core Web Vitals for SEO

To optimize Core Web Vitals and enhance UX, consider the following strategies:

1. **Page Speed**: Improve page speed by optimizing images, leveraging browser caching, and minimizing JavaScript and CSS files.

2. **LCP Improvement**: Ensure that the largest element on your pages loads quickly by optimizing images and content delivery.

3. **FID Enhancement**: Optimize JavaScript code and minimize render-blocking resources to reduce input delay.

4. **CLS Minimization**: Prevent unexpected layout shifts by specifying image dimensions, avoiding intrusive pop-ups, and using responsive design.

5. **Mobile Optimization**: Prioritize mobile optimization, as Core Web Vitals apply to mobile as well as desktop.

6. **Testing and Monitoring**: Use tools like Google PageSpeed Insights and Google Search Console to test and monitor your Core Web Vitals scores.

User Experience Best Practices

In addition to Core Web Vitals, consider these UX best practices:

1. **Mobile-Friendly Design**: Ensure your website is responsive and functions well on mobile devices.

2. **Intuitive Navigation**: Create a clear and intuitive navigation structure to help users find content easily.

3. **Readable Content**: Use legible fonts, appropriate font sizes, and sufficient line spacing to enhance readability.

4. **Engaging Design**: Implement an attractive and engaging design that aligns with your brand.

5. **Accessible Content**: Make your content accessible to all users, including those with disabilities. Use alt text for images, provide transcripts for videos, and follow accessibility guidelines.

6. **Clear Call-to-Actions (CTAs)**: Use clear and compelling CTAs to guide users toward desired actions.

Measuring UX and Core Web Vitals Success

Track your website's UX and Core Web Vitals success with the following metrics:

1. **Core Web Vitals Scores**: Monitor LCP, FID, and CLS scores using Google's tools.

2. **Bounce Rate**: Analyze your website's bounce rate to determine if users are engaging with your content.

3. **Time on Page**: Measure how long users spend on your pages, as it indicates their level of engagement.

4. **Conversion Rates**: Track conversion rates for specific actions (e.g., form submissions, purchases) to assess the impact of UX improvements.

Common UX and Core Web Vitals Pitfalls

Avoid these common pitfalls when optimizing UX and Core Web Vitals:

1. **Ignoring Mobile Optimization**: Neglecting mobile users can result in poor UX and lower search rankings.

2. **Heavy Page Elements**: Large images and excessive use of multimedia can slow down page loading times.

3. **Intrusive Pop-Ups**: Pop-ups that disrupt the user experience can negatively impact CLS.

User Experience and Core Web Vitals are integral to SEO success. By prioritizing a user-friendly website, optimizing for Core Web Vitals, and continually monitoring and improving the user journey, you create a foundation for higher search rankings and a more engaged audience. Remember that UX optimization is an ongoing process to keep your website competitive and user-focused.

Bonus Chapter:
The Power of SEO - Statistics and Why It's Your Best Ally

SEO (Search Engine Optimization) is not just a marketing strategy; it's a game-changer for small businesses aiming to succeed in the digital world. In this bonus chapter, we'll explore some compelling statistics that highlight the significance of SEO and why it's your best ally for online success. Plus, we'll guide you on where to find expert assistance.

The SEO Advantage - By the Numbers

1. **92.07% of Global Web Traffic**: According to StatCounter, Google dominates the search engine market share, making it the primary source of organic web traffic.

2. **75% Don't Scroll Past the First Page**: A study by Backlinko reveals that around three-quarters of users never scroll past the first page of search results. Ranking higher dramatically increases your chances of being seen.

3. **53.3% of All Website Traffic Comes from Organic Search**: BrightEdge research emphasizes the vital role of organic search in driving website traffic, outperforming other channels like paid search and social media.

4. **SEO Leads Have a 14.6% Close Rate**: SEO-generated leads have a significantly higher close rate compared to outbound leads (2.7%). (HubSpot)

5. **61% of Marketers Say SEO is Their Top Priority**: As reported by Databox, SEO is the leading focus for marketers, reflecting its importance in online strategies.

6. **Local SEO Delivers Results**: 88% of local business searches on mobile devices either call or visit the business within 24 hours. (Nectafy)

Why SEO Is Your Best Ally

- **Cost-Effective**: SEO offers a cost-effective way to attract organic traffic without the ongoing expenses of paid advertising.

- **Long-Term Results**: Unlike paid advertising, the results of SEO are long-lasting. Once your content ranks well, it can continue to drive traffic for months or even years.

- **Targeted Traffic**: SEO helps you attract visitors actively looking for your products or services, increasing the likelihood of conversions.

- **Brand Credibility**: High search engine rankings boost your brand's credibility and trustworthiness in the eyes of users.

- **Competitive Advantage**: Investing in SEO gives you a competitive edge, especially if your competitors are neglecting this essential strategy.

Get Expert Assistance

While the power of SEO is undeniable, it's also a complex field that requires expertise. If you're looking for professional guidance and support in your SEO journey, visit www.socialfunnelmarketing.com. Our team of experts specializes in helping businesses like yours harness the full potential of SEO to achieve online success. Don't miss out on the incredible opportunities SEO offers – reach out to us today and take your small business to new heights in the digital landscape.

Thanks for reading and we hope this guides you in your local SEO.

www.ingramcontent.com/pod-product-compliance
Lightning Source LLC
Chambersburg PA
CBHW051406250726
48656CB00006B/2294